AWESOME ANIMAL HEROES

TEMPLE GRANDIN

REBECCA FELIX

Consulting Editor, Diane Craig, M.A./Reading Specialist

Super Sandcastle

An Imprint of Abdo Publishing
abdopublishing.com

abdopublishing.com

Published by Abdo Publishing, a division of ABDO, PO Box 398166, Minneapolis, Minnesota 55439.
Copyright © 2017 by Abdo Consulting Group, Inc. International copyrights reserved in all countries.
No part of this book may be reproduced in any form without written permission from the publisher.
Super SandCastle™ is a trademark and logo of Abdo Publishing.

Printed in the United States of America, North Mankato, Minnesota
102016
012017

Editor: Paige Polinsky
Content Developer: Nancy Tuminelly
Cover and Interior Design and Production: Mighty Media, Inc.
Photo Credits: AP Images, Dedham Country Day School, iStockphoto, Laura Wilson, Rosalie Winnard, Shutterstock, Steve Jurvetson/Flickr, Wikimedia Commons

Publisher's Cataloging-in-Publication Data

Names: Felix, Rebecca, author.
Title: Temple Grandin / by Rebecca Felix.
Description: Minneapolis, MN : Abdo Publishing, 2017. | Series: Awesome animal
    heroes
Identifiers: LCCN 2016944659 | ISBN 9781680784343 (lib. bdg.) |
    ISBN 9781680797879 (ebook)
Subjects: LCSH: Grandin, Temple--Juvenile literature. | Animal scientists--
    United States--Biography--Juvenile literature. | Animal specialists--United
    States--Biography--Juvenile literature. | Women animal specialists-- United
    States--Biography--Juvenile literature. | Autistic people--United States--
    Biography--Juvenile literature.
Classification: DDC 636.092 [B]--dc23
LC record available at http://lccn.loc.gov/2016944659

Super SandCastle™ books are created by a team of professional educators, reading specialists, and content developers around five essential components—phonemic awareness, phonics, vocabulary, text comprehension, and fluency—to assist young readers as they develop reading skills and strategies and increase their general knowledge. All books are written, reviewed, and leveled for guided reading, early reading intervention, and Accelerated Reader™ programs for use in shared, guided, and independent reading and writing activities to support a balanced approach to literacy instruction.

CONTENTS

ANIMAL ADVOCATE

Temple Grandin is a scientist and a **designer**. She is a teacher too! Grandin is best known for her work with pigs and cattle. She teaches people how to raise these animals **humanely**.

Temple Grandin

TEMPLE GRANDIN

BORN: August 29, 1947, Boston, Massachusetts

MARRIED: never married

CHILDREN: no children

EARLY LIFE

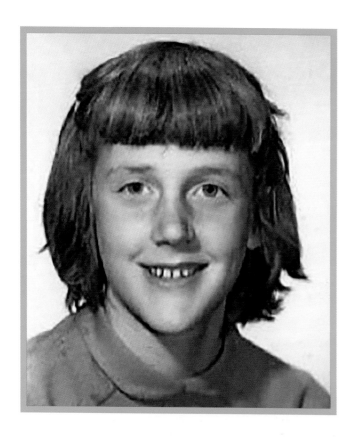

Mary Temple Grandin was born in Boston, Massachusetts in 1947. Her parents were Richard and Anna Eustacia. When Temple was two, doctors said she had brain damage. But this was incorrect. Her parents later learned Temple had **autism**.

Boston, Massachusetts

LEARNING TO SPEAK

Autism made it hard for Temple to speak. Her parents sent her to a special school. Temple finally spoke at about age four. But she had trouble making friends. Kids teased her in school.

Temple went to Dedham Country Day School. It is in Dedham, Massachusetts.

Temple (back row, third from left) *with her classmates at Dedham Country Day School*

ANIMAL BOND

Young Temple loved herd animals, such as cows and sheep. These animals become easily **stressed**. They do not understand words. Temple understood these behaviors. Her **autism** made her feel stressed too. And it made her think in pictures, not words.

Temple lived at her aunt's ranch for one summer. She spent a lot of time watching the cows.

SQUEEZE MACHINE

Tight stalls called crushes keep cattle still. This lets farmers check their health.

As a teen, Temple invented a "squeeze machine." Farmers used a similar machine to calm their cattle. Temple would lie in her machine. She pulled the padded sides tightly around her. The squeezing calmed Temple.

photo by Laura Wilson

DEGREES AND DESIGN

In college, Grandin studied **psychology** and animal science. She began working with livestock. Later, Grandin taught farmers how to treat their livestock well. She **designed** more comfortable handling systems for them.

At Arizona State University, Grandin studied squeeze machines used on cattle.

BUSY BUSINESS

Cattle can be scared by simple things, such as waving flags. Grandin helped cattle owners find and remove these things from their farms.

People took notice of Grandin's work. **Slaughterhouses** hired her to **design** their plants. In 1975, Grandin started a business. It is called Grandin Livestock Handling Systems. She has designed farms and plants across the nation.

Grandin visited farms and **slaughterhouses**. She studied their operations carefully to see what could improve.

SPEAKING OUT

Grandin became a public speaker. She spoke about animal **welfare**. Her methods are now used by many livestock workers. Today, Grandin teaches animal science at Colorado State University.

Grandin travels the country speaking about animal welfare and autism.

Grandin has taught at Colorado State University for more than 20 years.

LIVING LEGEND

Grandin changed the way livestock is treated. She made life more comfortable for millions of animals. And she is still hard at work. Grandin teaches young animal scientists to treat animals **humanely**. She inspires people to see animals differently.

Today, farmers across the world use cattle systems invented by Grandin.

MORE ABOUT GRANDIN

Grandin's SQUEEZE MACHINES are also called hug boxes. Some have been placed in schools. They are used to calm **autistic** children.

Grandin has a great VISUAL MEMORY. She is able to remember pictures very well.

A movie about Grandin's life was made in 2010. It is called *TEMPLE GRANDIN*. The movie won many awards.

TEST YOUR KNOWLEDGE

1. What disorder does Grandin have?

2. Grandin works mainly with wild animals, such as tigers. True or false?

3. What subject does Grandin teach?

THINK ABOUT IT!

What is your favorite farm animal? How is it similar to you?

ANSWERS: 1. Autism   2. False   3. Animal science

GLOSSARY

autism – a developmental disorder that affects communication and social relationships. Someone who has autism is autistic.

design – to plan how something will appear or work. Someone who plans how something will appear or work is a designer.

humane – kind or gentle to people or animals.

psychology – the science of the mind and behavior.

slaughterhouse – a building where animals are killed for their meat.

stressed – to feel mental or emotional strain or pressure.

welfare – the state of being happy, healthy, or successful.